THE NO-NONSENS

Read *How to Make Personal Financial Planning Work for You*

- If you want to learn how to set and meet financial goals
- If you want to learn how to analyze your financial needs
- If you want to learn how to organize and maximize your assets
- If you want to plan for big future expenditures—a house, vacation or college

NO-NONSENSE FINANCIAL GUIDES:

How to Finance Your Child's College Education
How to Use Credit and Credit Cards
Understanding Treasury Bills and Other U.S. Government Securities
Understanding Tax-Exempt Bonds
Understanding Money Market Funds
Understanding Mutual Funds
Understanding IRAs
Understanding Common Stocks
Understanding the Stock Market
Understanding Stock Options and Futures Markets
How to Choose a Discount Stockbroker
How to Make Personal Financial Planning Work for You
How to Plan and Invest for Your Retirement
Understanding Estate Planning and Wills

NO-NONSENSE REAL ESTATE GUIDES:

Understanding Condominiums and Co-ops
Understanding Buying and Selling a House
Understanding Mortgages

HOW TO MAKE PERSONAL FINANCIAL PLANNING WORK FOR YOU

Phyllis C. Kaufman
& Arnold Corrigan

LONGMEADOW PRESS

How To Make Personal Financial Planning Work for You

ISBN: 0-681-42104-5

Printed in the United States of America

0 9 8 7 6 5 4 3 2 1

To Gilman Kraft, with deep gratitude
and affection

ACKNOWLEDGEMENT
The authors gratefully
acknowledge the extensive
information and thoughtful
advice provided by Circle Consulting
Group, Inc. of New York

TABLE OF CONTENTS

TABLE OF CONTENTS

1

WHAT IS FINANCIAL PLANNING?

Although it may not be apparent from the title, this is a book about personal freedom.

What has freedom got to do with financial planning? A great deal. Almost all of us live under financial pressures of one type or another. And financial pressures are often the most persistent and difficult concerns we face. Even people who have enough money worry about whether they're managing it correctly, and where their money really goes.

It's hard to feel free when you don't know how much money you have, when you don't know whether you're doing the most with it, and when you don't know how much you really have to spend. Financial planning is a step toward understanding and freedom. It can help you put financial worries aside so that you can concentrate your energies on your family, your job, your home, and everything else in life that's important to you.

What is financial planning? It is a process of setting long-term economic (and psychological) goals and planning the financial steps needed to reach them.

The goals have to be reasonable in relation to your life situation, and the planning has to be done in a coordinated, organized way that looks not only at the goals but at the problems you may face in reaching them.

All of us sometimes plan financial matters. We sit down and think about buying a house, or about the children's education, or about whether to spend for that fabulous vacation, or whether to carry more life insurance. But we do these things piecemeal, one step at a time, with each step separate and not coordinated with the others. Often we solve one problem and find later that in doing so we have created or neglected others.

Very few people sit down, on their own, to review their financial affairs thoroughly and regularly, In fact, doing that is not as easy as it may sound. Relatively few people know how to go about it, and most people recognize that they don't have the knowledge to do it as well as they should. The professionals who they hope will help them—accountants, lawyers, insurance agents, stockbrokers, and other—often are trained to see only one part of the problem. And sometimes the professional sees even that one part from his or her point of view rather than from yours.

Emotions also get in the way. People sometimes won't look at their financial situation coolly and carefully because they're afraid of what they'll see. At the other end of the scale, some people are sure that they have more than enough money for all their needs, and see no point in sitting down to see if that really is true.

A whole new profession of *financial planners* has developed to help people plan their financial affairs in an organized and effective way. We'll talk later about when a professional planner may be right for you. But even if you should be getting help from a professional, the process has to start with *you,* and it won't work well without substantial thought and effort on your part.

So let's get you involved in financial planning. We think you'll be surprised at the new ideas and opportunities it will open up.

2

FINANCIAL PLANNING—AN OVERVIEW

So far we've been talking in generalities. What financial planning is all about will be clearer if we talk about the major problems that planning can help you solve.

We've said that planning has to start by setting long-term goals. Some goals are shared by many people—buying a house, financing children's education, saving for a comfortable retirement. Others may be a bit more special—planning for a vacation home, planning to set up a business, etc.

Think and Talk

What we do know is that many people haven't really thought about or communicated their goals. How do we know? Because when a husband and wife talk together with a professional about their goals, it often turns out that one is surprised to find out what the other's goals are. So the planning process begins with a thorough discussion and listing of goals. (See Chapter 4.)

Calculate

Next, consider the resources you have to help you get to those goals. First, what are your assets? Make a list of everything you have of financial value—house, cash, bank accounts, investments, insurance policies, etc. It will be important to list everything you can think of;

family assets that may not seem important to you may turn out to be very useful.

Where Does Your Money Go?

Next, on to the question and the part of the planning process that most people find the most troublesome of all: Where does the money go?

You may or may not be surprised to learn that most people *don't know* where it goes. The average individual or couple generally understands what money comes *in* to the home every week or month. But very few have a precise idea of how it gets spent. You can't plan how to make the best use of your money in the future unless you know how you are using it right now. So an absolutely essential part of the planning process is to draw up what some financial planners call a "cash flow" analysis—a business term that describes when and where the money goes.

Cash Flow Analysis

The cash flow analysis is hard work, as we shall see in Chapter 5. But if you're serious about getting rich, or about your children's education, or about saving up for an African safari, here is where you have to begin.

Don't expect it to be fun. After you have pulled all the figures together, you probably won't enjoy finding out how much you really spend on lunches at the office, or how much those charming dinners at the local bistro add up to over a year. Remember that, as a famous philosopher said, knowledge is power—even though at the moment it may feel depressing.

The cash flow analysis may show you some immediate steps to take if you don't want to be sailing in a financially leaky boat. Some of these may be things you knew you should have done all along, but you couldn't get yourself to do them until you saw the bleak figures down in black and white. For example, if you have no money in the bank, you'd better look over your expenses to see where you can cut down at least temporarily to build up cash—or think hard about finding a way of earning extra money until you have an emergency fund in place. Or, if you're spending a lot of money every month paying off credit card debt at 18% interest, perhaps seeing how much it really costs you will inspire you to cut down on some of those expenses, or to look for ways of consolidating your debts at a lower interest rate.

The cash flow analysis gives you ammunition you need to move to other steps and to go intelligently, where necessary, for professional help. The first step will probably be a careful review of your income taxes. Why? Because income taxes take a big slice out of the average individual or family income flow—because most people pay more taxes than they need to—and because the tax area is where good planning may most quickly turn up ways of saving cash in meaningful amounts.

Many people are under the impression that financial planning consists only of tax planning and tax savings. That isn't true—but tax planning is one of the key elements in the process, and perhaps the most important, because the potential dollar savings are so great.

The cash flow statement also lets you look at another key area more intelligently—your insurance. Until you know what you or your family normally spend, you can't begin to calculate how much life insurance you should be carrying for the sake of your dependents, or how much disability insurance for both your sake and theirs.

What next? In examining your taxes, you'll probably have looked at ways of putting money away for the future that are partly or wholly sheltered from taxes. The next step might be a total review of your investments. If you have invested for the immediate tax benefits and still have additional money available to invest, you'll want to make sure that those investments are being wisely managed, and that they tie in with your long-term objectives.

If you have a family or expect to have one, you'll have to take into account your children's education. College costs have skyrocketed over the last decade, and the only way to put children through college without financial agony is to plan carefully and to start early.

Where do you live? Whether you rent or own can be an important part of your planning process. If you own a home, it's a financial asset that you may or may not be managing most effectively.

Are you planning for your retirement? If not, why not? No matter how young you are, this is an area where the earlier you start, the better the results will be. But if you start late, the tax laws may give you possibilities of catching up of which most people are unaware.

Considering Your Job

In all the above, your job and the kind of work you do are critical elements which have to be taken into account. If you work for AT&T and expect to work for them for another 30 years, your planning will obviously be different than if you are self-employed, or prone to switch jobs, or working in a climate where people frequently get fired. And one part of the planning process is to examine very carefully the retirement and insurance benefits you have on your job. Surprisingly enough, most people have only a vague idea of what "fringe benefits" they have, even though these benefits are absolutely critical to how you will come out financially over the long run.

The last major element in your financial planning is estate planning—arranging what will happen to your assets when you are no longer around to enjoy them. Just as the financial planning process prepares you to deal productively with an accountant on your tax problems, it should prepare you to deal productively with a lawyer on making a will and planning for those you love.

Financial planning is the art of seeing all these problems in a connected, disciplined way so that you can deal with them better. Financial planning is not magic. It requires work on your part. If your income is limited, it can't suddenly give you luxuries and security. But it can often get you to goals you thought were out of reach, and help you make the most of your financial potential.

Perhaps most important, financial planning can give you the *sense of freedom* that comes from understanding your own situation and feeling confident that you are doing the most you can with it.

3

YOUR FINANCIAL PLANNING TEAM

This book will help you begin to take a professional approach to financial planning.

But you won't be a professional. Far from it. And even serious and responsible financial planners don't claim to be able to touch all the bases. They work with other professionals who are specialists.

If you have millions of dollars, you'll probably do your financial planning with a whole team of specialists. If you're in a low bracket, you'll have to do more of your financial planning yourself. (Your choices will be simpler, and you probably *can* do much of it yourself.) But in either case, you should know the professionals who may be helpful and who may relate, in one way or another, to the planning process.

Accountants

Accountants have many functions. You probably think of them primarily as the professionals who give income tax advice and do income tax returns. They vary greatly in helpfulness. We'll talk about them more in relation to taxes in Chapter 8.

Tax Attorneys

An experienced tax attorney will be more skilled than the average accountant in helping you plan broadly for tax reduction. For upper-bracket taxpayers who can use tax-sheltered investments, a good tax attorney is a necessity. (Some accountants function in this dual capacity.)

Insurance Agent or Consultant

The idea of "financial planning" as a professional function was probably originated by insurance people some years ago. In the good old days, the insurance agent who came to your house in the evening held himself out as an expert on your long-term financial needs and therefore qualified to sell you insurance. The approach wasn't illogical, though whether the agent was well enough qualified, let alone impartial, is another story. Today, the majority of the people who call themselves financial planning professionals have a background in insurance, and many of them still make their living basically as insurance salespersons. Yes, an experienced insurance agent may give you some useful financial planning help, but listen cautiously, and never forget that he or she is selling insurance.

Stockbroker

When stockbrokers give advice on investments, as most do, they are operating somewhere on the boundaries of financial planning—though certainly not every investment fits into a logical financial plan. Brokers are required by law to "know their customer," so that the advice will be appropriate to the client's individual situation. In fact, as we will note later on, more and more major brokerage houses are giving some of their brokers elementary training in financial planning and dubbing them financial planners. Will they give you sound advice? Perhaps. Will some of them be helpful? Yes. Can you trust them to be impartial? No.

Investment Advisers

Investment advisers who function only as advisers, and not also as brokers—that is, they are paid only for giving you advice, and not for selling you products or executing transactions for you—may be able to take a broader and more impartial view of your problems than the average stockbroker. Conversely, many financial planners give advice on specific investments. There's no legal requirement yet for registration of planners as there is for financial advisers, but the government is trying to make sure that any planners who give specific investment advice register under the law as investment advisers.

Banker

Bankers as financial planners? We're not referring to the fact that a few banks, like the stockbrokerage firms mentioned above, are putting employees through courses where they emerge with a "financial planning" emblem. We're thinking rather of the fact that a good banker is an expert on credit—personal loans, credit cards, mortgages, education loans, etc.—and that intelligent use of credit is one of the key ingredients in good financial planning. So if you are on good terms with a banker, he or she may be helpful to you.

Also, bankers have frequent contact with accountants, attorneys, and other professionals, including financial planners. If you are looking for professional help in one of these other fields, that banking friend of yours may be able to come up with helpful recommendations. It can't hurt to ask.

Oh, Yes—Financial Planners

No, we haven't forgotten the financial planners. They'll be mentioned throughout this book, and in Chapter 16, after you have gained a clearer idea of what you are looking for, we'll give some advice on finding a planner who is right for you.

4

WHAT ARE YOUR GOALS?

Most people feel instinctively that they know what their long-term goals are—better housing, more luxuries, education for children, a comfortable retirement, and other things.

So why make a list? First, while you may feel that you know your goals, it's surprising how often the process of putting them down on paper can lead you to recognize goals you'd been neglecting, or a different organization of priorities.

Second, for any two people living together—or even for a whole family, if the children are old enough to take part in the planning process—setting down goals can hold some special surprises. It's vital for spouses to launch into this part of the planning process *together*, and it's very common for at least one of them to find that the other's priorities were different than he or she had assumed. That's not a catastrophe, but it's obvious that people can't work out their differences unless they know what they are.

Third, with goals that require money (as most do), you can only plan for the goal if you translate it into dollar figures and also specify how much time you have to get there.

Fourth, getting your financial future in order requires discipline, which nobody likes very much. As long as you keep your goals vague, your efforts to get to them are likely to be vague too. It's only by putting down goals and setting a game plan that people can discipline themselves to save regularly and to take the time and effort needed to get their financial house in order. A clear effort requires a clear purpose.

What are your goals? There are some goals that are shared by everyone, regardless of family situation:

1. Everyone needs to put their current cash situation in order, to make sure there's an adequate emergency fund in the bank (or somewhere), to make sure the cash is earning interest at a reasonable rate, and to make sure they aren't using credit wastefully.

2. Everyone needs to make sure they are not paying more income tax than necessary, and that their tax situation is being managed as well as it can be.

3. Do you rent or own? In either case, you need to be sure that your housing arrangements are the best for you from a financial point of view.

4. Check your insurance arrangements. If you have no dependents, perhaps you don't feel you need life insurance. But do you have enough insurance against becoming disabled? You also need adequate medical and property insurance.

5. Everyone shares the goal of wanting to be financially comfortable later on in life—the period we usually refer to as retirement. It's a goal that's usually reached through several different investment and planning routes.

6. Beyond what's specifically needed for retirement, everyone wants to build up whatever wealth possible through saving and investment. And everyone wants to do this in a way that won't be eaten up by inflation.

7. Even if you have no dependents—even if you have no relatives—you need to have a will to make sure that your assets will go where you want them to. If your assets are large, you need careful estate planning to minimize the tax bite.

Once you have dependents, your will has to be adjusted, and some new goals have to be added:

8. You need to carry life insurance, planned carefully so that your dependents will be taken care of financially if you die.

9. If you have children or expect to have them, you need to plan financially for their education.

And finally we come to the goals that depend on your own preferences and your own living situation— as many of them as you want, and we hope you enjoy making the list:

10. Getting a new job, or being free to switch jobs. (Requires a cash reserve, provision to replace any job benefits you are giving up, and possibly an investment in education.)
11. Setting up your own business.
12. Building cash to start a family.
13. Buying a first home, or a new home.
14. Providing for aging parents.
15. Planning for luxuries:
    a. Vacations.
    b. Bigger car.
    c. Vacation home.
    d. Wine cellar.
    e. Boat.
    f. Fur coat
       etc., etc.

Have you made your list in writing? After you have ordered your priorities, you should write the number of years you have to plan before you need or hope to achieve each goal. Some items, of course, like tax reduction and disability insurance, need to be dealt with immediately. Others can be many years off. You can set up your table somewhat as we have done in the following table.

Goals to Plan For

	Years Away	*Amount Needed*
Liquid emergency fund	1	$ _____
Cash for adequate insurance	1	_____
New home (down payment and closing costs)	_____	_____
Remodeling home	_____	_____
New baby	_____	_____
New car (down payment)	_____	_____

Education
  Child #1 _____ _____
  Child #2 _____ _____
  Child #3 _____ _____
Starting a business _____ _____
Vacation home _____ _____
. . . etc. _____ _____

To help you think about future goals that require planning and saving now, we also show you a second table. This table shows how much you have to put away today to have $1,000 in the future—say 10, 20 or 30 years from now—at different assumed interest rates (that is, rates at which the money might grow if invested).

Investment Needed Now to Grow to $1,000

Years to Goal:	Annual Growth Rate				
	6%	8%	10%	12%	15%
5	$747.26	$680.58	$620.92	$567.43	$497.18
10	558.39	463.19	385.54	321.97	247.19
15	417.27	315.24	239.39	182.70	122.89
20	311.80	214.55	148.64	103.67	61.10
30	174.11	99.38	57.31	33.38	15.10
40	97.22	46.03	22.09	10.75	3.73

Why comment? The figures speak for themselves. As the saying goes, great oaks from little acorns grow. So even if you only have acorns now, and if your list of goals looks out of sight, take heart and keep reading.

5

MARSHALING YOUR RESOURCES, ARRAYING YOUR CASH FLOW

Now for some more lists. As we told you, financial planning requires an effort on your part. The next lists you will need are accounts of what you own and what you owe, with rough dollar amounts. The list of what you own may look something like the first table on the next page.

Obviously, some items may require several lines, while others may not apply to you at all. Next you need a matching table of what you owe, which will look something like the table list on the next page.

If you subtract your total debts from your total assets, you arrive at a figure termed your *net worth*. If your debts are bigger than your assets, your net worth is negative. Many people, especially younger people, have a negative net worth. It's not necessarily anything to worry about, but it's an extra reason why you should go through the financial planning process. But if you find that your net worth is getting smaller every year, or if the negative figure is getting bigger, it means that your debts are growing faster than your assets, and you should be concerned.

The next step is to prepare a cash flow analysis (also called a statement of income and outgo or simply a budget). This may take more time and effort than almost any other step in the planning process, but it is absolutely essential.

The reason it will probably take time and effort is that most people *have very little idea where the money goes*. That's true at all income levels. Let's hope you

Assets—What I (We) Own

Liquid Assets $
  Cash
  Bank accounts
  Bank CDs
  Money market funds
  Life insurance cash values   _____
    Subtotal
Investments (current market value)
  Stocks
  Bonds
  Mutual funds
  Other   _____
    Subtotal
Retirement plans (current value)
  Company pension plan
  Company profit-sharing plan
  IRA
  Keogh plan
  Annuities (cash value)   _____
    Subtotal
Business interests   _____
Personal property (current value)
  Home
  Second home
  Auto(s)
  Furniture
  Jewelry, furs, clothing
  Other   _____
    Subtotal   _____
GRAND TOTAL $

Debts—What I (We) Owe

Mortgage(s) $
Auto loan(s)
Instalment debt
Credit cards and charge accounts
Bank loans
Other loans
Margin debt on investments
Other   _____
  TOTAL $

are one of the exceptions, but in any case, to know whether your goals are realistic and how you can meet them, the first requirement is to know where your money is going *now*.

There are many different ways of setting this up. We like a simple 3-column setup, with one column for annual totals, and columns for weekly and monthly figures. The annual column must be filled in for each category; the weekly and monthly columns are to be used whenever convenient, both to let you see clearly how much you are spending and to arrive at the annual totals. A sample might look something like the following table.

It's an easy form to use. For some items, like auto insurance and vacations, you'll probably find it easiest simply to put in annual totals. For items that you usually think of in terms of weekly totals, such as food, put in the weekly figure and multiply by 52 to get the annual figure; for items that are usually paid monthly, such as rent, enter the monthly figure and multiply by 12.

If you haven't done this before, you will almost certainly have to track your cash expenses carefully for

Household expenses

	Weekly	Monthly	Annual
Rent (or mortgage)	$	$400	$4,800
Elec. & gas		80	960
Food	100		5,200
Household	20		1,040
Meals out	35		1,820
Entertainment	20		1,040
Clothing		100	1,200
Vacations			1,500
Gasoline			
Auto insurance			
Life insurance			
Tuition			
Etc., etc. . .			

at least a month, and perhaps for a few months, before you can complete the table accurately. Some days, when the cash remaining doesn't match the expense record, you may have to do a little detective work. Payments by check are of course easy to tabulate, and don't forget to include payments by credit card as well. In the case of checks and credit cards, you'll have to backtrack for 12 months to pick up the important items that may only be paid once or twice a year.

Tabulate your yearly income the same way, and make sure that your cash flow statement accounts for where your income goes, not down to the last penny or even to the last dollar, but at least within 5% and, if possible, within 2%.

The Budget Fall-out

What has the budget done for you?

If you are in a high-income bracket, you've probably confirmed that you're spending more money than you realized on many items that may or may not be important to you. As you work on your financial plan, you'll see whether or not this spending conflicts with reaching your longer-range goals.

If your income is average, the budgeting process may help you recognize different kinds of problems. What if your present ordinary living expenses consume the weekly or monthly paycheck, and there seems to be no room for meeting longer-run objectives? Financial planning can't create money out of thin air, but as we go along, you'll find suggestions to make the money pinch less burdensome. And if you go over your cash flow figures carefully, you may find areas that leave room for improvement.

Budgeting Together

Working out your cash flow is so critical to the financial planning process that it's essential for people married or living together to do it together. There may be some difficult discoveries, and the cash flow record certainly will be the basis for making some hard choices and decisions.

But two people who have *not* worked out their finances previously, and who have worried that expenses were too large, or savings too small, may find that putting the figures down in black and white together is a liberation. It opens the way to shared decisions and a shared approach to problems. Not everyone will take that opportunity, but with the figures in front of you, the way is open.

Just because a couple should do their planning and budgeting together—and we repeat that they should—doesn't mean that their money has to be commingled. The pattern is up to you. Some two-income couples keep bank accounts and expenditures completely separate, and some one-income couples similarly manage everything separately after dividing the paycheck on some agreed basis. Some couples put everything in the same pot and draw on it together.

It's a matter of preference. Obviously, if you tend to have arguments over who spent what and whether it was worth it, it may be wiser to allocate the money at the beginning and let each partner take it from there. You may spend a bit more on bank account charges, but the peace of mind could be well worth it.

6

CASH

One of your first objectives should be to have an adequate cash reserve.

What is adequate? Planners generally recommend that the cash reserve be enough to cover between two and six months' expenses. Two months might suffice for a couple with relatively secure jobs and no children. If the jobs are less secure and the family responsibilities greater, a bigger reserve is needed.

The guidelines obviously are vague, and you have to calculate just what your needs would be if you lost your job, or if there were sudden medical emergencies. And to the extent that you have other investments that you could turn into cash, the size of your cash reserve becomes less critical. But you don't want to be forced to sell your old General Motors stock just when the stock market is at its lowest point in five years.

Where should you keep the cash? A money market fund may be a good choice for high interest and for convenience in writing large checks, while a separate smaller bank account can be used for smaller checks. Figure out how many checks you generally write a month and what average balance you want to keep, and ask your bank representative to recommend a type of checking account. A bank money market deposit account will give you rates very close to those paid by the money funds, but the minimums often are $2,500 or more, which may or may not suit your needs. Shop around. (And read *Understanding Money Market Funds*.)

Consider, as an alternative, setting up one of the asset management or cash management accounts now offered by certain banks and brokerage firms. The minimums are often $10,000 or more, but certain brokerage firms (shop around) have lower requirements. These accounts let you earn interest on your checks until the check clears, and you can time your mailing of checks to earn interest until the last possible day or two. (Over the course of a year, this can save you more money than you think.) The accounts also may let you code your checks by category, which helps your cash flow record-keeping.

7

BORROWING AND SAVING

This chapter is short, but the point is important.

We've talked about the importance of building up a cash reserve. We'll be talking about the importance of *saving* for many of your financial goals. We had you draw up a calculation of your financial position in which every debt was subtracted from your net worth.

Yet also, in this book, we'll talk about *borrowing* as one of the important tools for achieving your financial goals (and, often, ultimately to *increase* your net worth). Is there a contradiction here? Some people think that debt is intrinsically bad, and the less the better. What approach makes sense?

If you manage it well, borrowing can be one of the most powerful financial tools you have. Borrowing is favored by the tax laws. When you borrow, the interest you pay is tax-deductible.* Borrowing also is favored by the way the economy works. Inflation has pushed up the price of real estate and other real assets over the years, and the trend is likely to continue. When you borrow to become an owner, you enjoy the gain from inflation, while you pay the debt back later with dollars that are worth less, and enjoy the tax deduction on the interest you pay in the meantime.

Borrowing almost always makes sense when it's for a productive purpose. When you buy a house, or a condo or co-op, borrowing is usually essential. Borrowing (prudently) lets you increase your investments for the future. It can let you make tax-advantaged invest-

*Tax proposals introduced in 1985 would limit this deduction, except for mortgage interest on your principal home.

ments that decrease the taxes you owe. If you already own a house, you can borrow on it to finance other investments, such as education, etc. All these make good sense.

Borrowing to pay for current expenses, or for luxuries, is a very different matter. Here you are paying interest to enjoy the expenditure earlier rather than later. Even if you get a tax deduction, is it worth the interest? If you save and make the purchase later, you will *earn* interest on the money while you save. And if this kind of debt mounts up, there's no house or investment nest egg at the end to help pay it off. (For more information, see *How to Use Credit and Credit Cards.*)

When you borrow to buy an asset and pay off the loan with regular payments, you have really set up a useful arrangement for forced saving. Paying off a mortgage loan is one of the most widespread forms of forced saving in the U.S. At the end, you have paid off the mortgage and you own the house—often more valuable than when you brought it—free and clear.

Where borrowing makes good sense and the terms are reasonable, you should probably borrow even if you could make part or all of the payment in cash. Why? Because another important tool in the financial planning process is *cash*, and you should be building up as much as you can. Cash gives you the ability to make a down payment on a house, condo or co-op, and to begin to enjoy the tax and other advantages of home ownership. Cash lets you make investments which will reduce your taxes and ultimately increase your wealth.

When you are borrowing on a house, a car, or on investments in order to save your cash, you can earn income on the cash and offset at least part of the interest paid on the borrowing. Even if it doesn't quite match, remember that keeping the cash gives you flexibility.

Of course, if the tax laws are changed so that the interest on your borrowing is only tax-deductible up to a certain maximum, all borrowings will have to be looked at with extra care. But you still would have substantial room to take advantage of the deduction.

8

YOU AND YOUR TAXES

After looking at your assets, debts, and cash flow, the first thing a good financial planner will ask to see is your last few income tax returns.

Many people are under the impression that financial planning consists solely of tax planning. That's a misunderstanding. But because people pay so much in income taxes, that is the prime area where planning helps to improve your cash flow and build up your assets. And, as we will see, tax considerations affect many of the other areas where a good financial plan functions.

Let's start with your tax return. A large number of Americans pay more taxes than they need to, simply because they don't take advantage of all the possible deductions. If you do your own tax return, take time to read carefully the IRS instruction book *Your Income Tax* (a gold mine of suggestions, and free from the IRS) or one of the standard commercial tax-assistance publications. If you don't itemize deductions, take time to do the calculation and see whether itemization might help you. If you find that your tax return has become complicated enough to puzzle you, consider going to an accountant for professional help.

However, if you are using an accountant now or planning to use one, don't expect the accountant to do all the work. You have to do your share. A good CPA (certified public accountant) will certainly know how to take all the information you provide and produce an effective tax return from it. But what about the receipts you forgot to save, the deductions you forgot to mention, the items you didn't know were deductible?

In particular, many people aren't aware that if you itemize, expenses related to your job and your investments are deductible, and there's no doubt that millions of taxpayers miss out on sizeable deductions that could be taken in this manner.

A professional financial planner will do two things that a good accountant probably won't take time to do. First, the planner will look carefully at your job, cash flow statement and lifestyle in order to search (with your help) for additional tax deductions and credits. Second, the planner will make suggestions as to how you could *change* some of your actions and habits in order to save on taxes.

A good CPA probably knows how to make the same suggestions. But clients pay CPAs for doing tax returns and usually don't expect to pay for the extra time that would be needed for the CPA to act as a planner. Besides, many of the best CPAs are primarily involved in auditing, business accounting, or other activities, and doing individual tax returns is often a low-priority item. Your accountant may be glad to work in conjunction with a financial planner, and in fact many of the better financial planners get a good proportion of their clients through accountant referrals.

Company Benefit Plans

One source of tax savings that many people don't exploit effectively is company benefit plans. With someone—perhaps your company benefits officer, perhaps an accountant, perhaps a financial planner—you should review the fringe benefits available to you on the job, and see whether you are taking advantage of them. Retirement plans may let you put aside extra savings with advantages. (See Chapter 12 and, for more information, *How to Plan and Invest for Your Retirement*.) If you are at a higher executive level, a good financial planner will help you negotiate for a benefits package that will work to your best advantage.

9

TAX SHELTERS

Many people think of financial planners and tax shelters as being completely intertwined. It's true that finding tax-sheltered investments for high-bracket clients is one of the main activities of many people who advertise themselves as financial planners. But there's a question as to how many clients really get what they pay for.

What Is a Tax Shelter?

The concept of a tax shelter is simple enough. To oversimplify drastically, say that you buy a share in a real estate development which calls for you to invest $10,000 each year for three years ($30,000 total) in the "limited partnership" which is the legal form used for the investment. In each of these three years, your share of the partnership's expenses for depreciation, interest and property taxes amounts to $16,000. Since you are in a 50% tax bracket, you save $8,000 in taxes each year (50% of $16,000), and so the net cost of the investment to you is only $2,000 per year, or $6,000 total. Let's assume that after two more years your share can be sold, not for the $30,000 originally invested, but for $18,000. Compared with your net cost of $6,000, you have tripled your money (a 200% profit before taxes). Even allowing for the time your money has been tied up, it's a good deal.

But what if the real estate development isn't successful? Or what if it's an oil and gas drilling venture, and the managers come up with too many dry holes? In that case your $6,000 may become worthless rather than doubling or tripling, and you will have taken a real loss and not just a tax loss.

The Dangers of Tax Shelters

What makes the tax shelter area risky for the average investor is that shelters have become a popular marketing item. There's a big public demand for them, but there isn't a big enough supply of high-quality shelter investments to satisfy the demand, and the novice can't tell the good from the bad.

Where to Find Good Tax Shelters

Many of the better deals are distributed privately through accountants, lawyers, and other professionals. Bankers often have access to interesting deals. If your income is $125,000 or $150,000 or more, tax-sheltered investments may carry great advantages for you, and you may also have enough cash available to participate in prime deals that may require $50,000 or $100,000 as a minimum.

What to Look For

If you walk into a brokerage office off the street and ask for tax shelters, you'll be offered items probably of lesser quality that permit smaller investments. If you're tempted to go into any of these, read the offering prospectus very carefully and make sure you get the answers to the following questions:

1. Is the investment valid apart from the tax benefits?
2. Will there be any secondary market where you can sell your share later on, if you wish?
3. How much do the insiders—the managers, promoters or general partners—have invested? Do they stand to lose significantly if the deal turns out poorly, or is all the risk on the public investors?
4. What share of the profits do the insiders take? Is it in proportion to their investment?
5. What are the fees and commissions? How much of your money is really working for you after all deductions?

The Risks

Whatever you do, don't invest before you get a second opinion from your lawyer or accountant. Remember that if a tax-sheltered investment turns out badly, you face a double risk. You can lose part of your investment; and the IRS may use the bad results to argue that the investment had no "valid economic purpose" (the acid test), that it was therefore only a tax gimmick, and disallow all your tax deductions.

As you can see, there are risks.

A Different Approach

Because many commercial tax shelter deals are disappointing, some accountants and planners suggest that the middle-income person looking for tax relief take a different approach. First, your own home may be the best tax shelter available, and any individual or couple not already owning their own house, condo or co-op should immediately begin thinking about buying one if at all possible.

Second, consider the possibility of other local real estate investments. You may not feel able to judge values and prospects in your area, but you should be able to find an attorney, accountant or banker (or all three) whom you trust and who are experienced in real estate properties. A small, well-chosen rental property can give you tax write-offs for depreciation, mortgage interest and property taxes and still serve as a valid long-term investment that will provide a real buildup in value.

What If You're Short of Cash?

What if you're in a fairly high tax bracket but none of the tax-sheltered investments we have discussed seem possible because you're short of cash? You may be advised to borrow in order to buy into a tax-sheltered investment. Strictly on the numbers, the tax savings may seem to justify the borrowing. But tax shelters generally involve risks of some degree, and if you have to borrow to make the investment, it probably means that you shouldn't be making the investment at all.

More on Tax Planning

As we have said, tax planning is a pervasive aspect of financial planning, and we have only touched on a few facets of it. Some other points will come up in later chapters. Insurance, investments, planning for children's education, planning for retirement—all involve taking advantage of some of the tax breaks the law allows.

One final point. For upper-income persons, one of the standard planning techniques is that of shifting income to other members of the family who are in lower brackets. In Chapter 14, we'll mention shifting of income to children through outright gifts or by other means. Remember that if you have other dependents—perhaps parents for whom you want to provide—the same techniques apply. Your accountant and attorney can easily help you review the possibilities.

10

YOUR HOME

No matter how much you love your home, don't be afraid to think of it also as a valuable financial asset—almost certainly one of your most valuable—which should be one of the cornerstones of your financial planning.

We've touched on this in earlier chapters. For most people, *owning* a home is an essential step if they want to make the most of their living and tax arrangements. You may be one of the exceptions—perhaps your job requires frequent moves that make home ownership difficult. But in most circumstances, anyone who doesn't own a house, condo or co-op should be thinking seriously about it; and if your problem is that you can't afford the down payment, you should waste no time in starting to save.

For many Americans, buying a home is the biggest single investment they will ever make, the mortgage loan will be their biggest single borrowing, and paying off the mortgage, as we mentioned earlier, will probably be one of their most effective methods of forced saving.

If your income is limited, mortgage payments may seem like a financial burden. But with time, or with added income, the situation may change. And if, as often happens, the house appreciates in value, your situation will be changed importantly for the better.

Look at your situation in a new way. You are the owner of a valuable asset—your house. This asset gives you valuable borrowing power which you would not have had otherwise, and you can *manage* this borrowing in ways that will do you the most good.

Refinancing

Assuming that you have paid your mortgage down, or your house has risen in value, or both, you can *refinance* your mortgage, that is, take out a new mortgage, in this case for the purpose of increasing your borrowing capacity. You'll probably have to go through the same procedures and costs you originally incurred in getting the mortgage loan—credit check, appraisal, title search, attorney's costs, etc.—but if the new mortgage is with the same lender as the old, it may be possible to short-cut some of this.

Second Mortgage and Equity Credit Lines

If your old mortgage is at a favorable rate, you may want to leave the old mortgage in place and to add a second mortgage. In the past, second mortgages generally have been on rather expensive terms to the borrower. Now a new alternative has been developed— equity credit lines, which are more flexible and which are the latest and "hottest" way of unlocking the extra credit power in your house. Banks, brokerage houses and others have jumped on the bandwagon.

The lender puts you through a full mortgage check (which, you should note, might cost you about 3% of the amount you expect to borrow) and then gives you a line of credit which may be good for five years or perhaps indefinitely. The amount of the credit line might be figured as follows: Say that your house is appraised at $100,000, and your lender's practice is to lend up to 75% of the appraised value—in your case $75,000. But you still owe a balance of $45,000 on your old mortgage. The lender subtracts this and arrives at $30,000 as your net line of credit. You can borrow up to this amount whenever you wish, and you pay interest only on the actual amount borrowed.

It's a flexible and highly useful arrangement. But a few warnings. First, make sure you understand all the rules and costs. Second, make sure you understand how the interest rate will be set when you borrow. Third, make sure you have a long repayment period, comparable to a mortgage—some of the banks will permit 25-year repayments, but some of the brokerage houses have plans which call for much faster repayments. Read the fine print.

Finally, don't enter into this arrangement without remembering that *the lender has a lien on your house.* This isn't just a personal loan—it's the equivalent of a mortgage. Make sure that your borrowing is for a good purpose and that you can repay what you borrow, before you put your house at risk.

Having given these warnings, let us point out the many purposes for which you might want to draw on your home for extra credit. The new mortgage or the equity line might give you the cash you need (but don't have) for a purchase of additional real estate property as we suggested in Chapter 9. You may find other investments which will return more, over the long run, than the cost of the borrowing (but consider these other investments very carefully before you borrow). You may need cash to finance your children's education—perhaps immediately, perhaps for the kind of future preparations that we will discuss in Chapter 14. You might want to make a down payment on a vacation home. Or, finally, if you are loaded with credit card debt and personal loans at rates of 18% and above, you might use your home equity to clean up this "junk debt" and consolidate your debt into one home equity or mortgage loan at a substantially lower rate.

All of these are steps which can carry specific dollar advantages for you, and which are part of your financial plan. But of course, saving dollars isn't everything—you might want to use your loan or credit line simply to make improvements or additions to your present home. That's legitimate too.

11

INSURANCE

Everyone recognizes the importance of insurance—also referred to as protection against catastrophe, risk management, etc. But very few people have a clear idea of just what kinds of insurance, and in what amounts, they should carry. Strangely enough, most people don't even have a clear idea of what insurance they are carrying now.

If that last statement sounds questionable, remember that for most individuals and families, the fringe benefits package they have through their job represents an important part of their insurance coverage—and most people have only a hazy idea of what their fringe benefits really cover. Exactly the same applies to the insurance coverage that almost everyone has through Social Security. Finally, people usually buy individual insurance through an agent or salesperson, often on the agent's recommendation as to which policy is best. As in all financial planning matters, if you don't take the time to work through the numbers yourself, it's hard to understand what you need or what you have.

As we said earlier, the majority of people who call themselves financial planners come from the insurance industry, and insurance agents who don't formally carry the financial planner title still often think of themselves as involved in financial planning. Many of these individuals are quite knowledgeable. Still, when you buy insurance from someone who makes a living selling it, it pays to do your homework carefully and to review all the alternatives before you sign on the dotted line.

Knowing Your Fringe Benefits

In planning your insurance coverage, the first step is to know what your job covers. The situation varies tremendously from company to company—from no benefits at all, to packages which take care of a substantial part of your insurance needs.

A typical package may include a modest amount of life insurance (group insurance, a form of term insurance—see below); Blue Cross-type insurance to cover hospitalization expenses, and probably some major medical insurance against other medical costs; workers' compensation insurance, which covers against any injuries on the job; and possibly some disability insurance.

Know your benefits. Get them in writing from the company benefits officer, and have him or her explain fully any points you don't understand. Show the package to your insurance agent and/or your financial planner, if you have one, and discuss it fully. Make sure you know what you have, and get the best advice you can on what's still missing.

Social Security

Social Security resembles company fringe packages in that people know they have it, but don't know what's in it. The original part of Social Security was the *retirement benefits* that normally begin at age 65. But Social Security also includes *survivors' benefits*, which are a special form of life insurance, helpful especially if you leave children under 18 years old; insurance in case of *permanent disability;* and now, also, *Medicare*, which provides broad health insurance coverage for those over age 65.

Your coverage depends on your age, how long you have worked in employment covered by Social Security, and how much you earned while so employed. The benefits are modest, and you need to supplement all of them with other coverage, but they are still a valuable base. As with your company package, the first rule is: know your coverage. Go or write to your local Social

Security office and ask for the basic booklets which will let you estimate your coverage in all the above areas. Take the figures with you when you talk to your insurance agent (who should know how the Social Security benefits work—but don't count on it).

Life Insurance

Life insurance is a key tool in financial planning, and it has several purposes. The first purpose, of course, is to protect your dependents if you die. It's not hard to find life insurance policies that will accomplish that. But choosing among the variety of policies that are offered can be hard indeed, and your insurance agent is not in a good position to give you impartial advice.

Types of Life Insurance

Years ago, traditional life insurance policies generally combined a pure insurance element—for payment of benefits if you die—with a savings element. At one time, these were the primary savings programs of many individuals. Because the savings element builds up a cash value (or "surrender value"), these are called "permanent" or "whole life" insurance.

Then, two things happened. First, people began to realize that their life insurance premiums were going for both savings and insurance, and that it might be better to separate the two. Many people began to buy primarily *term* insurance, that is, pure life insurance with no savings component, and do their savings elsewhere.

Second, group insurance became an important part of many people's insurance coverage. And group life insurance is term insurance, without any savings component.

People turned to term insurance because the life insurance companies generally don't give you a very good deal on savings. In traditional policies, the accumulation rate may not be generous, and there are sizeable deductions for commissions and expenses. However, as we will see below, the new *universal life* policies generally give you a better break in these respects. This is worth noting.

35

Insurance carries some important tax advantages, and policies with a savings element can play an important part in financial planning: planning:

1. These policies act as an income tax shelter. The interest on your cash value accumulates free of income tax. (Tax reform proposals introduced in 1985 may eliminate this privilege.)
2. The policies are a form of forced saving, which some people need. And if you need the cash value, you can borrow against your policy.
3. Life insurance has a special place in estate planning. We won't go too fully into the technical details here, but if the insured person has carefully given up ownership and control of the insurance policy to another individual or to a trust, the proceeds of the policy are *not* subject to estate tax when the insured person dies. In an estate that is large enough to be subject to estate tax, this is a way to pass on a big chunk of money free from the tax. For this purpose, term insurance has a disadvantage in that the premiums on term insurance (where you are simply betting the insurance company on whether you will die) become very large after age 60 or 65 (when your chances of dying, and winning the bet, increase). If you want to have insurance in force until you die, it's less painful to take out a universal life policy, where the savings built up in the policy can pay the increased premium cost as the years go on.

Estate planning problems, of course, should be handled with the help of an experienced attorney. For now, let's go back to the question of basic life insurance to protect your family in case you die.

There's no simple way of setting guidelines about how much life insurance you need. You have to sit down and carefully work out a "family needs" analysis. Do you supply your family with income? Homemaking services? Both? If you die, how much annual income will they need to live comfortably? Are there other sources of income that will help? How much will be added by Social Security and company benefits?

What is the net annual amount that has to be added by private insurance? How big a policy is needed to produce that much annual income?

Once you've answered these questions, you're ready to talk to an insurance agent. Term life insurance will be the cheapest way to get coverage. Or, turning it around, if the maximum amount you can spend is limited, term insurance will give you by far the largest policy for your dollars.

However, if you can afford bigger premiums, and see merit in some forced saving, consider the new universal life policies. In effect, competitive pressures have forced the insurance industry to come out with a more flexible product. You can view the universal life product as somewhat like a term policy plus a savings element in the form of a tax-sheltered money market fund investment. Commissions on these policies are generally lower than on the old whole life policies. There is unusual flexibility in the amount of premium you can pay each year, and you can, in effect, use the tax-sheltered earnings on the money market segment to pay the insurance premiums. As the professionals like to put it, you are paying your insurance premiums with "pre-tax dollars," i.e., with income on which you don't have to pay income tax. Are you in a 50% tax bracket? Then your tax saving amounts to 50% of the amount of the premiums. It's a worthwhile break.

Disability Insurance

One of the favors this book will do for you is to make you think about disability insurance (also termed disability income insurance).

To put it bluntly, if you are under 50 years of age, your risk of becoming permanently disabled in any nearby year is five or six times as great as your risk of dying. Few people know this and few people carry adequate insurance against it.

Some disability insurance policies protect you for longer periods, some shorter. Some pay you if the disability prevents you from following your usual occupation; some pay you only if you are totally disabled and can't work at all. The commercial policies are likely to be structured so that they pay you about 60% of your normal income; in the case of policies where you pay the premium yourself, this is better than it sounds, since the benefits from those policies are generally tax-exempt. (The benefits from company-paid policies generally are not.)

Social Security only pays you benefits if you are defined as totally disabled, so it may not be prudent to count on it. If you have coverage through your company, study the policy carefully; find out just how large the benefits will be and for how long. Then draw up the same kind of "family needs" analysis that you did in the case of life insurance.

If you find that you need disability insurance beyond what would be provided by your company policy (and possibly Social Security), talk to your insurance agent. You want a policy that gives a liberal definition of disability, and you want one that gives you long-term coverage, preferably to age 65.

But the more liberal policies are not cheap. If the cost forces you to compromise, you may have to take a policy that covers you for two years if you can't follow your usual occupation, but covers you permanently after that only if you are totally disabled and can't work at all. (After the first two years, if you can work at *any* job, the insurance coverage won't apply.)

Health Insurance

There are so many different types of health insurance policies available that we will discuss them only in the broadest terms. Many people have substantial health coverage on their jobs, and don't bother to look further; obviously, it pays to look at your company policy carefully to see if it needs to be supplemented.

If you are self-employed or otherwise have no health coverage provided to you, you might do well to consider membership in a health maintenance organization (HMO) as an alternative to traditional health insurance. An individual or family pays the HMO a fixed fee each year, and the HMO provides doctors and hospital services as required. Since the doctors are employees of the HMO, the patient-doctor relationship is far from the traditional one. But the HMO seems to be a possible way of delivering satisfactory medical care at definitely lower cost.

If you are shopping for an HMO, the problem is that some seem definitely to be better than others. Pick one that has been in operation long enough to be tested, and before you sign up, talk with a few of the members to find out what their experience has been.

Property and Liability Insurance

If you are a home owner or tenant-renter, you need (and probably already have) one of the several standard policies that protect you against theft. You should also have personal liability insurance, to insure you if someone is injured in your apartment, home or on your property. Home owners also need insurance protection against fire, storm, and other natural damage.

The details of these policies are outside the scope of a book on financial planning, but we'll mention a few key points:

1. If you are an owner, make sure that your home is insured for *at least* 80% of its replacement value. Otherwise your recovery for any loss will be reduced, even if it's for a partial loss that appears to be within the limit of the policy. Review your coverage every year to see if it needs to be increased.
2. Draw up a list of your personal property with estimates of the replacement value of each item. Keep a copy of the list somewhere away from your home, where it will be safe and available in case of disaster. Update the list carefully every year or two, and make sure that your insurance on these items also is increased as needed.
3. If your policy covers you for personal liability only up to $25,000, as many still do, spend whatever modest extra amount is needed to raise the cover-

age to at least $100,000. Even when the inflation in everything else is brought under control, the inflation in lawsuits continues. You may also want to consider an "umbrella" policy. For a small yearly premium, you can get excess liability coverage of $1,000,000 or more.

Insurance, You, and Your Financial Planner

In this chapter we've assumed that you are your own financial planner and that you will deal with your insurance agent (or perhaps several insurance agents) as intelligently as possible. The more carefully you prepare your figures and questions, the better your results.

But of course, much depends on the insurance agent too. A knowledgeable agent who believes in putting the client's needs first can be a great help. Unfortunately, there seems to be no easy rule for finding that kind of agent or broker. You should ask your lawyer for recommendations—and your accountant, your banker, and anyone else you can think of. Ask the agent about his or her specialization, if any, and experience. If the agent carries the designation CLU (chartered life underwriter) or CPCU (chartered property casualty underwriter), it's evidence of extra study and experience, though that doesn't prove that he or she will put your interests first. Ask the agent what kinds of programs he or she would recommend. Ask in particular for advice about term insurance—a type of insurance that definitely helps you more than it does the agent. Ask for references and, when you follow them up, see if you can find anyone who has had to deal with the agent on a difficult claim matter. Be patient until you find an agent with whom you feel comfortable. Remember that getting the best policies at lowest cost could, in case of catastrophe, make an important lifetime difference to you and your family.

What if the insurance agent is a financial planner? Much the same rules apply. The planner is functioning here as a salesperson, and the title doesn't tell you the one thing you need to know: whether the individual will put *your* interests first.

If you are working with an independent planner separate from the insurance agent, the situation is of course completely different. The planner will review all the above matters with you and help you work out exactly what insurance is needed in your own situation. Although the planner may not want to encroach on the territory of the insurance agent, he or she should be able to send you off to the fray armed with models of desirable policies, and with guidelines as to what the premiums should be.

You'd rather not pay two professionals for the same job? We don't blame you. But sometimes two end up being cheaper than one.

12

PLANNING FOR RETIREMENT

You might think that planning for retirement would be one of the last subjects to be taken up in financial planning. Actually, it is one of the first. And the investments you make that are aimed at retirement are among your first investments.

Why? One reason is that there are important tax advantages in retirement investing that you want to take advantage of immediately. Second, in investing for retirement—and this is just as true of any kind of investing—your investment compounds more rapidly as the number of years grow, and the sooner you get started, the better.

Besides, the knowledge that you have a secure retirement ahead of you can do more than almost anything else to give you freedom and peace of mind, which is what financial planning is all about.

Your retirement planning rests on four foundations:

1. Your company retirement plan or plans.
2. Social Security.
3. Your IRA—and your Keogh plan, if you are self-employed.
4. Your investments outside these formal retirement plans.

The different ways in which you should plan and invest for retirement deserve a separate book—and we recommend to you *How to Plan and Invest for Your Retirement*. Here we point out some of the major factors you should be concerned with, and how these tie in with your total financial plan.

Your Company Retirement Plans

There is no legal requirement that a company have any sort of retirement plan. But if a company has such a plan or plans, the law says that certain rules must be followed to protect employees and avoid discrimination. And plans above a certain size that promise specific benefits must contribute to the government's Pension Benefit Guaranty Corporation, to make sure that the benefits are paid as promised.

The most common type of company plan is a *defined benefit pension plan.* "Defined benefit" means that on retirement, employees are promised a certain specific scale of benefits, often calculated in relation to the employee's salary level in the last years before retirement. Age and length of service are also usually taken into account. It's estimated that the average defined benefit plan starts a retired employee off at about 40% of pre-retirement income. The employer is responsible for putting enough money in a trust fund each year so that the benefits can be paid when due.

There are also *defined contribution* plans. Here the employer makes contributions into the plan according to certain rules, but no specific benefits are promised. Your benefits depend not only on how much has been put in the plan for your account, but also on how it has been *invested* and how successfully the money has grown. In some cases, the employer keeps full control over how the money is invested; in other cases, the employee has a choice.

The defined contribution plans may include a *profit-sharing* plan, where the company has complete flexibility as to how much to contribute each year, and/or a *money purchase pension plan,* where the company commits itself to contribute a certain percentage (for example, 10% or 15%) of each employee's compensation each year.

Another form of defined contribution plan is the *salary reduction plan,* now widely known as a *401(k) plan.* In this, employees have the option of having part of their compensation put directly into a profit-sharing plan rather than paid to them as wages or salary. Because the amount doesn't appear as salary, the employee pays no income tax on it. Often, the company may "match" part of the contribution. There are also similar salary reduction plans, known as *403(b) plans*, for employees of educational institutions and certain nonprofit organizations.

Integration with Social Security

Company retirement plans are often "integrated with Social Security," a help if you are higher-income, but not an advantage if you are lower-income. It means that the company's contributions are relatively lower on that part of an employee's pay that is taxed for Social Security, and relatively higher on the part of pay above that level. In 1985, the "maximum covered wage" for Social Security" was $39,600. So in an integrated plan, a relatively smaller percentage would have been contributed on the first $39,600 of an individual's pay, and a relatively larger percentage on any pay above that level. Obviously, individuals with total pay of more than $39,600 benefitted from this arrangement—the higher the income, the more the relative advantage.

The Tax Advantages

People often take the tax advantages of all these programs for granted, but a moment's reflection shows that they are exceptional. You pay no income tax on the money the company puts in the plan, and once in the plan the money is invested and builds up *tax-free* until retirement. This permits the ultimate benefits to be high relative to the contributions. (When you retire, you *do* pay income tax on the benefits as you receive them.)

Knowing the Plan

Here, just as with company insurance benefits, it's important to know clearly how your company's retirement plan(s) work. Some of the many questions to ask are:

- Which employees are covered?
- When do employees join the plan?

- How are contributions determined? Are they integrated with Social Security?
- Are employees required to contribute to the plan?
- How are benefits determined?
- When are benefits vested? (Vesting means that benefits become attached to an employee so that the employee can't lose them even if he or she leaves the company.)
- If benefits are vested, but the employee leaves the company before normal retirement, does he or she get the benefits in a lump sum payment to take along, or do they stay in the plan until the employee reaches normal retirement age (wherever he or she may be)?
- Can you retire early? If so, what is the reduction in benefits?
- Can you borrow from the plan, or withdraw money early in case of hardship?
- If it's a defined benefit plan, how are the benefits adjusted for inflation?
- If it's a defined contribution plan, how is the money invested? (This may be the most important question of all.)

These are some of the key questions. (For more, see *How to Plan and Invest for Your Retirement.*)

Obviously, the possible variations are overwhelming. But it's essential that by yourself, or with your company benefits officer, or with the help of an accountant, attorney, or planner, you review any retirement plans your company has until you are clear regarding what they mean for you.

Most of the above questions deal with what the plans can do for you in the future. But you should pay particular attention to the features that may make a difference to your planning *now:*

If your company has a 401(k) plan (or if you work where there is a 403(b) plan), are you putting in the maximum you can? If your dollars are limited and you have to choose between one of these plans and an IRA, these plans usually have even more advantages.

If your company makes "matching" contributions into a 401(k) plan or any other plan, are you putting in as much as you can to take advantage of this feature?

If you are fortunate enough to have more savings than you can put into an IRA, a 401(k), or any other plan that gives you a tax deduction, does your company plan permit what are called nondeductible voluntary contributions? These are additional contributions that you put into the plan from your own savings. You don't get a tax deduction for the contribution, but your money can grow tax-free in the plan, which is an important advantage. You have freedom to take your original money out again if you need it, though the earnings it has built up have to stay in the plan.

If you are permitted to borrow from the plan, what are the terms and how much is available? If the interest rate is reasonable, this can be one of the best sources of credit you have.

Most important of all, do you have control over how your money is invested? If so, remember that this is a powerful tool for your future. If the company has a profit-sharing plan that permits an investment choice between guaranteed interest rate investments and a growth investment such as a common stock fund, check whether the growth investment has a good past record and consider using it. (See the discussions below regarding IRAs and in Chapter 13.)

Social Security

Almost everyone who works for a living is covered by Social Security, and Social Security retirement benefits are an important part of your planning.

Among the many advantages of Social Security is that the benefits are completely portable, or "vested"—all the time. You don't have to worry about switching jobs, or breaks in employment, or other factors that can interfere with your coverage under company plans. Whether you have ever thought about it or not, your Social Security number is a modest but important ticket to job freedom and flexibility.

The Social Security rules are explained more fully in *How to Plan and Invest for Your Retirement*. Here we'll mention the highlights. The key to your Social Security benefits is "covered employment"—the number of years you have worked in jobs where you paid Social Security taxes. You need to have roughly 10 years of covered employment by retirement age (normally age 65, but it can be earlier or later) to qualify for retirement benefits at all.

The *size* of your monthly retirement benefits takes into account your long-term earnings record going back 25 years or more. If you have earned the "maximum covered wage"—the maximum amount subject to Social Security taxes—for many years, you will be entitled to the maximum monthly benefit.

This maximum is adjusted periodically for inflation. A worker retiring at age 65 in 1985, and entitled to the maximum benefit, would start receiving a monthly benefit equivalent to about $8,600 per year. If the worker had a nonworking spouse, the benefit would be increased by 50% to roughly $12,900. If both spouses have long working records, they could each be entitled separately to the maximum single benefit.

However, note that it's not as easy to earn the "maximum covered wage" as it used to be. The table that follows shows how the amount of pay covered by Social Security tax has changed over the years—and the percentage that has been taxed away from you.

Obviously, you won't retire rich on Social Security. But it's an important building block for your retirement, and you should know the rules. Ask your local Social Security office for their booklets explaining how retirement benefits and other parts of the system work. Also, fill out Form No. 7004, the "Request for Statement of Earnings," to find out your accumulated earnings credits. In addition, mark the form "Show Q/Cs" to get your quarters of coverage. If the system's computers have not followed you accurately from job to job—or, especially in the case of women, from one name to another—get the problem corrected and your earnings credited accurately at once, before you are on the verge of retirement.

Year	Maximum Covered Wage	Tax Rate	Maximum Tax
1950	$ 3,000	1.5 %	$ 45.00
1960	4,800	3.0	144.00
1970	7,800	4.8	374.40
1975	14,100	5.85	824.85
1976	15,300	5.85	895.05
1977	16,500	5.85	965.25
1978	17,700	6.05	1,070.85
1979	22,900	6.13	1,403.77
1980	25,900	6.13	1,587.67
1981	29,700	6.65	1,975.05
1982	32,400	6.70	2,170.80
1983	35,700	6.70	2,391.90
1984	37,800	6.70	2,532.60
1985	39,600	7.05	2,791.80

Making the Most of Your IRA

Almost everyone has become familiar with IRAs—Individual Retirement Accounts. An IRA is a vital part of your retirement planning and of your total financial planning. An IRA is a tax shelter for everyone who works for a living.

Let's hope that you are familiar with the IRA rules. We'll only mention the highlights. You can contribute up to $2,000 or 100% of your *earned* income, whichever is less, to an IRA each year. Earned income means wages, salaries, and other income you earn by your own current efforts; it does *not* include interest, dividends, pensions, etc. But in a special break, *alimony* is now regarded as earned income for IRA purposes.

The IRA gives you a great double tax advantage. First, you get an *income tax deduction* for the amount contributed, up to the permitted limit. Second, and even more important, your money *earns and compounds tax-free* in your IRA, and you pay no tax on the buildup until the money is withdrawn.

If two spouses work, each can have a completely separate IRA. If one doesn't work, a "spousal" IRA can be set up for that spouse, and the combined contributions to the regular and spousal IRAs can be up to $2,250.

You should know *all* the IRA rules, and we recommend that you read *Understanding IRAs*. Note that the above rules were as they stood in mid-1985, and that Congress at that time was being asked to raise the contribution limit on spousal IRAs, and perhaps to make other changes as well.

An IRA gives you great flexibility. If you can't afford $2,000, you can put in any amount up to that limit. You can begin taking money out without penalty at age 59½, but you don't have to begin taking it out until age 70½. You can start an IRA and have the money invested with all sorts of institutions including banks, brokerage firms, and mutual funds. You can have many IRAs and can split your money among different investments. And you can switch from one to another freely.

While you don't have to put in the maximum, the results of regularly investing $2,000 a year are remarkable. The following table shows how your IRA would build up at $2,000 a year, assuming investments at different growth rates from 6% to 15%. And just to show that it's worth your while even if you can only invest less, we've added figures to show what happens at only $500 a year.

There are some obvious lessons you can draw from the table—lessons, in fact, that apply to any tax-sheltered investment plan:

1. Start an IRA as soon as you can and fund it as early in the year as possible. See how the compounding effect accelerates over the years.
2. Keep your eye on the tax-free accumulation. Even in a year when you don't care about the tax deduction, get as many dollars into the tax shelter as you can.
3. Think carefully about your investments, and consider taking moderate risks by investing your IRA

Value at End of	Annual Growth Rate				
	6%	8%	10%	12%	15%
$2,000 per year:					
5 years	$ 11,951	$ 12,672	$ 13,431	$ 14,230	$ 15,507
10 "	27,943	31,291	35,062	39,309	46,699
15 "	49,345	58,649	69,899	83,507	109,435
20 "	77,985	98,846	126,005	161,397	235,620
30 "	167,603	244,692	361,887	540,585	999,914
40 "	328,095	559,562	973,704	1,718,285	4,091,908
$500 per year:					
5 years	$ 2,988	$ 3,168	$ 3,358	$ 3,558	$ 3,877
10 "	6,986	7,823	8,766	9,827	11,675
15 "	12,336	14,662	17,475	20,877	27,359
20 "	19,496	24,711	31,501	40,349	58,905
30 "	41,901	61,173	90,472	135,146	249,978
40 "	82,024	139,891	243,426	429,571	1,022,977

in growth investments such as common stock mutual funds. See, for example, how remarkably the difference between 8% growth and 10% growth multiplies over 20 or 30 years.

The advantages of an IRA make it, as we said above, the "tax shelter for everyone." For almost everyone, it should be a cornerstone of financial planning. But there are exceptions. If your company has a 401(k) plan and you absolutely can't afford both that and an IRA, the 401(k) plan should ordinarily take the edge—it has all the advantages of an IRA and some others as well. And if your company has any kind of plan where it matches your contributions, the same argument may apply. You need to work out the figures.

But try to build up an IRA in any case. It may even be worth it to borrow to make your contribution. Increasing the borrowing on your house in order to fund your IRA can work well in terms of saving taxes, though it's a step you shouldn't take without careful thought.

Keogh Plans

If you're self-employed, you can't have a company retirement plan unless you start one yourself. Keogh plans, or self-employed retirement plans, give you the opportunity for very large tax-deductible contributions and investments—as much as $30,000 per year or even more.

Keogh plans are complicated, and you should see your attorney or accountant about them. If you are self-employed with employees, the complications increase. But the very large permitted contributions give a Keogh plan like a far greater dollar potential than an IRA, with much the same flexibility and wide range of possible investments.

Having a Keogh plan doesn't prevent you from having an IRA—you can have both. And a Keogh plan can cover earnings from part-time self-employment. So if you work for a company and are self-employed part-time, you might easily have three retirement plans—the company plan, your IRA, and a Keogh plan. (For more information on Keogh plans, see *How to Plan and Invest for Your Retirement.*)

Your Own Investments

We said earlier that the fourth financial cornerstone of retirement planning is your investments outside any retirement plan. In the next chapter we'll turn to the general subject of your investments. First, though, a note on the *taxability* of those investments.

IRAs, Keoghs, and most company retirement plans are fully tax-sheltered. There's no income tax on the money going into the plan, and the money earns and accumulates tax-free as long as it's in the plan—with the kind of impressive results that we saw when discussing IRAs.

There are also certain investments where you don't get an income tax deduction for putting money in, but where the money does accumulate tax-free once invested. Permanent life insurance and deferred annuities are two of these (see Chapter 11).

Most other investments are thought of as not carrying special tax advantages. But all *growth* investments benefit from breaks the tax laws give to long-term capital gains. If you hold an investment longer than the required holding period (presently six months), any profit on the sale is taxed at only 40% of normal tax rates. Moreover, you don't pay a tax on the capital appreciation until the asset is sold; until then, the buildup in value is tax-deferred. We'll say more about capital gains investing in the next chapter.

13

PLANNING YOUR INVESTMENTS

If you're considering working with a professional financial planner, this chapter may be of particular importance to you.

The best financial planners often have backgrounds in law, accounting or perhaps in insurance. They are experts in helping you with the mechanics and tax arrangements (such as retirement plans) through which your money is invested. But when it comes to choosing the *actual investments* best suited for making your money grow over the long run, the planner may be less expert.

The planner may not have the specific training and background of an investment adviser. But even if he or she has that background, keep in mind that investing is as much an art as a science, and the results you have with professionals will vary greatly.

So even if you're using a qualified planner, do some thinking and reading about investments. If you're acting as your own planner, that's even more necessary.

Some Investment Principles

Investing generally involves a trade-off between risk and reward. The higher the reward you aim for, the greater the risks are likely to be. So in choosing investments, you need to examine your attitude toward risks and your willingness occasionally to put up with some uncertainty in the hope of reaping greater long-term rewards.

It's a mistake to think that you can avoid all risks by "playing it safe." Sometimes there are hidden risks in supposedly safe investments. Money in the savings bank can lose part of its purchasing power because of inflation. "Safe" bonds can drop in value because of a rise in interest rates. So try to train yourself not to be afraid of moderate risks. What's important is to *know* what the risks are, keep a careful eye on them, and don't hesitate to change your approach if you think that the risks may be out of proportion. Also, as your investments grow, limit your risks by *diversifying*—by spreading your money over several different investments so that if one proves disappointing, it won't seriously affect your whole investment program.

Income investments are generally considered more predictable and less risky than *growth* investments. An income investment is one where the value of your original investment either holds absolutely constant (as in a bank account or money market fund) or is expected to fluctuate only moderately, while a relatively predictable amount of income is added to the account every year.

A *growth* investment is one that you choose mainly because it is expected to rise in value—whether it be common stocks, real estate, or old comic books. Because there's no guarantee of growth, and because growth is hard to predict, the risks in these investments are obviously higher. If the investment isn't successful, your money may shrink rather than grow. Even if the investment does well, market values may fluctuate. But investors are willing to take these risks because *the best growth investments have built up people's money much faster than the best income investments.*

You have probably heard of the "miracle" of compound interest. If money is left to grow for long enough, the effect of compounding becomes spectacular. But it's also important to recognize that even a small difference in growth rates will make a great difference in long-run results. To show the effects of compounding, the table on the next page shows how an investment of $1,000 would build up at different growth rates over the years.

Another problem that you have to consider in your investments is *inflation*. Some investments help protect against inflation, others don't. Many growth investments have the advantage of protecting against inflation.

TABLE 8
How $1,000 Can Grow

Value at End of:	Annual Growth Rate				
	6%	8%	10%	12%	15%
1 Year	$ 1,060	$ 1,080	$ 1,100	$ 1,120	$ 1,150
5 Years	1,338	1,469	1,611	1,762	2,011
10 "	1,791	2,159	2,594	3,106	4,046
15 "	2,397	3,172	4,177	5,474	8,137
20 "	3,207	4,661	6,727	9,646	16,367
30 "	5,743	10,063	17,449	29,960	66,212
40 "	10,286	21,725	45,259	93,051	267,864

Basic Investment Choices

There are certain basic choices to make in your regular investments, in your IRA or Keogh, and in those company plans that give you a choice. To start with, the simplest income-type investments are bank accounts and certificates of deposit, and money market funds. These give you great safety and stability. Your dollars don't fluctuate at all, but earn regular interest which you can plow back into the account.

Since interest rates tend to rise and fall with inflation, if you plow your interest back into the account you should at least keep even with inflation, and perhaps a little ahead. You won't have spectacular results, but you won't have a disaster either. U.S. Treasury bills and notes give you the same general type of investment and basically similar results, sometimes with a slight edge in performance.

Bonds tie your money up for longer periods at a predetermined interest rate. Theoretically, if you keep plowing the interest payments back, you should stay comfortably ahead of inflation. But if the inflation rate rises sharply, the interest rate on your bond won't adjust, and you may regret the investment. In buying a bond, you're betting that the inflation rate won't get out of hand. It's a bet that carries a risk.

Common Stocks

Common stocks often pay regular dividends, but we think they are particularly important as *growth* investments—in fact, the growth investment most easily available to the average investor. Common stocks are shares of ownership in corporations—auto companies, oil companies, chemical companies, retail chains, etc. If a corporation is profitable and grows successfully, the value of its shares should increase. But there's no guarantee, and there are often many zig-zags along the way.

Common stocks adjust to inflation, because inflation makes the corporations worth more as the values of their properties increase—factories, forests, oil wells, land, etc. Common stock prices often seem out of step with inflation, running ahead in some years and falling behind in others. But if the stocks are well chosen, they can give you double growth—from inflation, and from the company's own growth and expansion. Over the whole postwar period, common stock investments kept investors, on the average, 6% to 7% ahead of inflation, a very nice margin. The average doesn't tell the whole story—some stocks did much better and others did much worse—but it shows the possibilities.

Real growth is growth after adjusting for inflation. If an investment grows in dollar terms at 15% a year, but the inflation rate is also 15%, the real growth rate is zero. Look at the 6% column in the table on page 56 to see how the *real* value of common stock investments has grown, on the average, over the years.

As we said above, common stock investments vary tremendously from good to bad, and *selection* is critical. Some stockbrokers and investment advisers have good records, but not all. If you don't know a broker or adviser with a proven record, you can solve the selection problem with *mutual funds*.

Why Mutual Funds?

A mutual fund is a way of pooling the money of many investors so that it can be managed efficiently and economically as a single large unit. Because the pool is large, the mutual fund can afford to hire high-quality *professional management*. It can also easily *diversify* its investments and reduce risks by spreading the total investment over many different securities.

Mutual funds are used more and more as investment choices in company profit-sharing plans, 401(k) plans, etc. For example, you might be able to choose whether to direct your money into a money market fund, a bond fund, or a common stock fund. You might also be able to divide your money among two or more choices, and to switch from one to the other.

The same approach is possible as a way of investing your IRA. Many mutual funds are "no-load" funds, meaning that you can buy shares without paying any commission. Over the years, well-selected no-load common stock mutual funds could be one of the best ways of making your IRA grow. (The same is true of your investments outside the IRA.)

Advising the Planners

In our experience, many (though not all) financial planners fail to appreciate the possibilities of common stocks, or the extent to which the risks can be managed through mutual funds. Some planners are more comfortable with types of investments where the results can be projected with more mathematical certainty. Some planners prefer investments which give specific tax savings initially.

Remember, as we discussed earlier, that successful growth investments carry their own tax shelter in the form of long-term capital gains tax treatment. And you are not limited to the particular types of investment (oil drilling, real estate, etc.) featured in many tax shelter deals. Over the long run, probably the greatest fortunes have been made by careful, intelligent selection of investments which have grown in value through the years, without help from special tax advantages or gimmicks.

14

PLANNING FOR EDUCATION

College costs worry everyone. If you have children now or expect to have them, preparing for college costs is an important part of your financial plan.

Most financial planners use computer programs to analyze data provided by their clients and to calculate specific recommendations in different areas. The savings-for-college problem lends itself to relatively simple computerized solutions. These shouldn't be taken too literally—some of the assumptions will surely change as time goes by—but they can help get you off to a reasonable start.

For example, say that Susan is now 10 years old and will go to college at age 18. At the college you hope she will attend, costs are now $14,000 per year, or $56,000 for four years; if you assume a 7% inflation rate, her total college costs for four years will be about $107,000. To cover these costs, you want to put away a steady amount each year (including the four years when she will be at college). If you assume that you can earn 12% annually on this college fund, you need to put aside about $6,100 per year beginning now, assuming that you will keep saving the same amount through Susan's senior year.

But remember that you are in a 40% tax bracket, and that the net tax on the earnings in your college fund will probably be around 25%. This cuts your yield, or growth rate, from 12% to 9%. So now, if you want the fund to cover you also for these income taxes, the amount you need to set aside each year rises to around $7,100.

In view of the expected inflation rate, you might

/ find it easier to put in less in the early years and more later on. The computer can do that too, but for simplicity we'll assume a level savings amount.

Obviously, you could save $900 per year if there were no income tax on the fund's earnings. One way of eliminating the tax, or at least reducing it, is to put the money under Susan's name and Social Security number, where no income tax will be owed until the earnings are large enough so that a separate tax return has to be filed under her name. The easiest and most popular way of doing this is to make gifts to Susan each year under the Uniform Gifts to Minors Act, which has been passed in all states. An adult acts as *custodian* for Susan, and separate "custodial accounts" are set up wherever you want the money invested. It's a simple procedure. There's no gift tax if gifts are limited to $10,000 from one parent or $20,000 from both.

But there are a few possible problems you should know about. First, you are giving up control of the money; it really belongs to Susan now, despite the custodian set-up, and it can't even be used to pay for items for Susan if those are support items that would normally be paid for by a parent. Second, when Susan reaches the "age of majority" (18 in most states), the money becomes hers outright, with no custodian. You'd better be sure that you can count on Susan to use the money for college and not for something else. Third, if the money will still be in the custodial account when Susan starts college, the courts have been raising questions as to whether college costs can be paid by such an account, as was always permitted in the past; you should keep in touch with your attorney or accountant on this point.

Another way of having the money taxed to Susan rather than to you would be by setting up a formal *trust* arrangement. For higher-income people particularly, attorneys and planners often recommend the use of a *Clifford trust* or a *spousal remainder trust* as a way of shifting income. Trusts are complicated legal documents, and you should consult with an experienced trust attorney if you want to explore these alternatives—especially since the tax advantages of these trust arrangements could be curtailed by Congress.

Start Early

The most important advice to be given in this whole area is: *start early*. We assumed that Susan is now 10 years old. With college costs what they are now, the time to start saving is the day you bring your new baby home from the hospital, if not before. If you had started your saving on the day Susan was born, with all the other assumptions unchanged, you would only have had to save annually about $1,500 (at 12%) or $2,100 (at 9%). The figures speak for themselves.

Of course, preparation for college involves much more than simply saving dollars. In the examples above, we've assumed that Susan gets no financial aid while at college. Of course, while she is at high school you will be exploring all her possibilities of obtaining grants or loans. If you know or think you know what college she will attend, talk to the college about special financing ideas. Many colleges will make creative suggestions. (For more information on this subject, see *How to Finance Your Child's College Education*.)

What if Susan gets to college and, with all your saving and all the (we hope) grants and loans, you're still short of money? Remember the equity in your home, and see if you can use an equity credit line to supply cash to fill the gap. (See Chapter 10.)

15

ESTATE PLANNING

Estate planning means planning what happens to your property after you die. It's a complicated specialty where you need the help of an experienced estate attorney. Not only will the attorney know the special tax and legal rules, but he or she will have the experience needed to help you fit your plan to your own situation and desires.

Having stressed that you need professional help, let us make a few comments. People often put off estate planning because they don't want to think about death. Nevertheless, we all die sooner or later; and if two people live together, one of them eventually will be left alone.

For everyone, it's important to make a will so that your property will pass to the ones you love (or to whomever you choose) as you intend. And it's important to go through a planning process to support the will, to make sure that assets will be there when they're needed, and to minimize the bite of federal and state taxes on the estate.

For two spouses, it's critically important to plan goals together so that each will have the knowledge to survive successfully alone.

As noted above, a critical part of estate planning is to eliminate or reduce estate taxes. To be subject to federal estate tax, an estate must have a value of over $400,000 in 1985, over $500,000 in 1986, and over $600,000 for someone dying in 1987 or thereafter. Amounts left by one spouse to another are not taxable, whatever the amount; but careful tax planning is needed so that there won't later be a big tax bite when the second spouse dies.

In the process of planning and drawing up your will, a good estate attorney will handle that problem and many others. The attorney will make sure that the ownership arrangements on your property are as they should be; will arrange your life insurance so that the proceeds aren't taxed to your estate; will make sure that your retirement plans are in order, with the correct designations of beneficiary; and will review dozens of other items. If your estate is large, the attorney will probably suggest that you consider transfers of assets during your lifetime.

The Role of the Planner

If you are using a financial planner, where does he or she fit into this?

A good estate attorney will take care of almost all your problems in this area. But a good planner can help. It may be the planner who points out in the first place that you have no will, or that your will is out of date, or that it was drawn by an attorney who is not an estate specialist (a danger in any case, but particularly if your estate is large enough to be taxable).

The planner may know you, or you and your spouse, better than the attorney does. The planner may discuss your goals and financial situation, and may prepare you better to work productively with the attorney.

Also, your planner is in a position to coordinate your estate plan with the other parts of your financial planning. He or she can help coordinate your investments, your insurance and your retirement planning with your estate plan.

16

USING THE PROFESSIONALS

Often in this book we've talked as if you were your own financial planner. Occasionally we've talked about using a professional.

What approach you take will depend in large part on your income bracket. Many highly qualified financial planners specialize in helping upper-income people for high fees. But financial planning has become a popular concept, and all sorts of services have blossomed, ranging down to computerized "plans" which you can obtain for as little as $100, or even for free.

Good Financial Planners—Can You Afford One?

As this book has shown, an individual or firm that wants to offer high-quality planning advice has to have expertise in many fields—taxes, accounting, law, investments and insurance. The planners who truly have this broad expertise generally work with clients on a consultation basis, producing extensive individualized plans for fees that start at $2,000 or $3,000 and range considerably upward. For clients with incomes of $150,000 annually or more, and assets of $300,000 or $400,000 or more, the fees may well be worth it.

The explosion of lower-priced financial planning services depends on the fact that information from the client can be fed into a computer to produce a plan full of projections and recommendations. The price generally depends on the extent to which this is accompanied by individualized services or not.

Brokerage firms, insurance firms, accounting firms and banks all have been getting into the act. Several of them offer a menu of services at different price ranges. For roughly $1,000 to $2,000 you can get plans virtually as detailed as those from the specialist planning firms mentioned above. For prices as low as $100 you can get a computerized plan with no service at all, produced from the personal financial data that you submit in writing.

Any of these plans may provide you with many useful suggestions and recommendations. But you can't rely on them for impartial advice. The people serving you, and the computer programs themselves, are oriented toward getting you to buy the products the firm is selling. These may include brokerage or insurance or other services. The danger, and it's a very real one, is that an impressive and authoritative-looking plan will get you to put money into items that may be of mediocre quality, or not suited to your situation, or both. For examples of what we mean, see the discussions of tax shelters in Chapter 9 and life insurance in Chapter 11.

That doesn't mean all these services are useless—if you do your homework, go in well informed, and recognize that you're dealing with people who have something to sell. Bank or brokerage personnel who have taken brief planning courses, and are trained to make relatively standard recommendations, may be doing some clients a favor. It can hardly be wrong to advise a client who doesn't have an IRA to start one, or to advise someone to save who isn't saving, or to tell someone to look more carefully for income tax deductions. Sometimes a small push, even from a non-expert, may get a client to do something he or she knew should have been done all along. But when specific products begin to be recommended, the best advice is—let the buyer beware.

Distorting the Process

The most basic criticism of the lower-priced services is that they distort the planning process. As we've seen, good planning advice should involve a continual back-and-forth between planner and client, a defining of goals, a discovery of ways to reach them that takes into account the client's particular job, family situation, risk preferences, etc. Even the best computer program can't substitute for the personalized advice that a good planner gives.

If your dollars are limited, there's a way to use these lower-priced, computerized services that makes sense. Shop around, and spend a few hundred dollars for the program that appears most balanced and inclusive. Use it in your planning. But don't trust it too far, and don't let it make decisions for you. *You* are the financial planner; it is only a tool. Even if the specific recommendations don't seem right for you, it may give you new approaches and ways of organizing your figures that more than repay the cost.

Good Financial Planners—Can You Find One?

If you have decided to spend for the services of a high-quality planner—how do you find one?

Throughout this book, we've implied that many of those who call themselves financial planners don't know as much as they should or aren't as impartial as they should be. Some planners know only one or two specialized areas well, while others are involved primarily in selling certain products.

Anyone can claim to be a financial planner. There's no clear definition, and no government regulation. A planner may be regulated in some other capacity, such as investment adviser, stockbroker, or insurance agent—but not as a planner, or at least not yet.

Some planners have received the designation of Chartered Financial Planner (CFP) from the College for Financial Planning in Denver, Colorado. The American College in Bryn Mawr, Pennsylvania gives a certificate as Chartered Financial Consultant (ChFC), and there are a handful of other colleges and universities that offer a range of courses in financial planning. Many planners are members of the International Association for Financial Planning (IAFP), a professional association. Some of these designations are useful in showing that a planner has had additional training in one or more aspects of the field. But in your search for a planner to work with you, it would be a mistake to give any of the titles too much weight.

What can count for more, very simply, are personal recommendations and interviews. Ask your attorney, accountant or banker for the names of any financial planners in the area that they can recommend strongly. Talk to other business associates and friends. Try to get more than one name.

Interview the candidates—even if you have to pay a consultation fee for the interview time. Ask about the planner's education, training and experience, and find out from what background (such as law, insurance, etc.) he or she came. Ask what type of client the planner serves. Ask for references from clients whom the planner has served for five years or more. Ask to see samples of plans given to clients, with names deleted.

Ask about fees, including both the fee for the first year and the (presumably lower) fees in subsequent years for review and follow-up. Ask particularly whether the planner works for fees only, or whether he or she earns commissions on sale of any products.

There's a keen continuing debate within the industry on the relationship of commissions and fees. The planners who work on a fee-only basis claim that any sale of products for commissions destroys the planner's ability to be impartial. Of course, there are many cases where this is true. But the opposite argument deserves to be listened to. All planners, including the fee-only planners, are often in the position of recommending that clients buy certain products on which substantial commissions are charged—notably tax shelters, certain other investment products, insurance and annuities. In many cases, the client will pay a commission wherever he or she goes to buy. If the client buys through the planner, the planner earns the commission and can compensate by charging somewhat lower fees.

In this case, of course, you are relying on the integrity of the professional. But the same is true of many other professionals with whom you deal. In planning, as in other fields, there are some honest professionals who believe that the way to build up a clientele successfully over the long run is to serve the client's best interests now. And there are professionals who are not so ethical. You'll have to make your own judgments.

One sensible course is to seek out a planner who seems to be so successful that he or she has no great need to make extra money off *you*. But in any case there's no substitute for getting personal recommendations and asking hard questions of the planner.

Once you have begun to work with a planner, there's one more test to apply. Does the planner work comfortably and well with your accountant and attorney, and perhaps with the other professionals you deal with? If not, find out where the problem is. If your accountant or attorney is too defensive to take valid suggestions, this is a good time to find out about it. If the planner is trying to encroach on someone else's territory, this is a good time to find that out too. Remember, in blunt terms, that you are the client and that you have the right to get the services you are paying for.

17

THE MOST COMMON MISTAKES

Financial planning covers a tremendously wide range of subjects and problems, and, if you are acting as your own planner, it may be hard to know where to begin. This book has tried to give you a sequence to follow. But it may help you to know what planning mistakes professionals say people most often make. If any of these describe you, you will have found good points on which to start:

- To take specifics first, most people pay too much income tax because they don't take all the deductions and credits they are entitled to.
- People also pay unneeded taxes because they don't take the time to learn about, and make, tax-advantaged investments.
- They don't have a will, or their will is out of date.
- Their life insurance is poorly planned and chosen.
- They spend too little on disability insurance, and often have the wrong type.
- They fail to know their company fringe benefits or to use them properly.
- They spend too much and save too little, for lack of clear goals and discipline.
- They don't think hard enough about their savings and investments, and they don't review them regularly.

As you can see, most of these failures are failures to *think*. Thinking is hard work, and it takes time. You have to *think* to set your objectives and to plan. But it's vitally important to start early, to organize your objectives, to plan far ahead, and to think in long-run rather than short-run terms.

It's also important to stay on your toes, financially speaking. Even the best plan has to be reviewed and updated regularly. Whether you have done your plan yourself or with a professional, make sure that you think about it every few months and that you give it a full review at least once a year.

September and October are good months to give your plan some extra thought. Hopefully, you are refreshed and rested from the summer. There's still time to take actions that might reduce this year's taxes. And it's not too early to begin thinking about next year.

The other months that are very good for planning are November, December, January, February, March, April, May, June, July and August.

18

FINANCIAL PLANNING FOR EVERYONE

We've said that a certain type of financial planner only serves high-income clients. And sometimes it sounds as though the whole profession revolves around tax shelters and other maneuvers designed only for high tax bracket individuals.

This book has tried to show that a limited picture of financial planning is wrong. The process of setting clear objectives and planning ways to reach them may be even more necessary for individuals or couples of modest means.

Financial planning is important because it teaches people to set clear objectives, teaches couples to work together in planning for the future, illuminates the possibilities and shows practical ways of achieving them.

Professional financial planners certainly help. But where that's not practical, people can do a surprising amount for themselves.

Age is no barrier to planning. Young people have time on their side, even if their income now is low. Money put aside, in an IRA or elsewhere, will have extra years to compound. Older people close to retirement may have missed some of the earlier opportunities, but may still be able to use the tax laws to make their retirement brighter and more comfortable.

Similarly, income is no barrier to making use of financial planning. If your income is low, setting up your budget and considering your objectives becomes even more important. The better you understand your situation, the better the chance of changing it. If this book helps even a few people change their lives for the better, it will have fulfilled its purpose.

About the Authors

ARNOLD CORRIGAN, noted financial expert, is the author of *How Your IRA Can Make You a Millionaire* and a frequent guest on financial talk shows. A senior officer of a large New York investment advisory firm, he holds Bachelor's and Master's degrees in economics from Harvard and has written for *Barron's* and other financial publications.

PHYLLIS C. KAUFMAN, the originator of the *No-Nonsense Guides*, has made her mark in a number of fields. She is a Philadelphia entertainment attorney, theatrical producer, marketing consultant and former dancer. She holds degrees from Brandeis and Temple Universities.